I0087973

Nesting

Nesting

A Collection of Poetry

Erin Ruzicka Trondson

© 2010, Erin Ruzicka Trondson

ISBN: 978-1-934074-54-1

All rights reserved. No part of this book may be reproduced or transmitted in any form or by any means, electronic or mechanical, including photocopy, recording, or any information storage and retrieval system, without prior permission from the publisher (except by reviewers who may quote brief passages).

Printed in the United States of America

First Edition

Published by Apprentice House
The Future of Publishing...Today!

Apprentice House
Communication Department
Loyola University Maryland
4501 N. Charles Street
Baltimore, MD 21210

410.617.5265
www.ApprenticeHouse.com
info@ApprenticeHouse.com

Acknowledgements

The author wishes to acknowledge the publications in which the following poems first appeared.

The Wrong Picture, *Connections*

Greener Grass, *So to Speak*

Nesting, *Cold Mountain Review*

Newborn Falling Asleep, *Canvas*

The completion of *Nesting* was aided by a fellowship at Edenfred and the arts residency of the Terry Family Foundation in Madison. The author is also deeply grateful to Cynthia Marie Hoffman and J.L. Conrad for their advice and guidance as she completed the manuscript.

For my husband and daughters

Table of Contents

To Settle 1

Close 2

Rising 3

Nesting 4

The Wrong Picture 5

Birth 6

Birth II 7

A Round 8

Sweet Milk Days 9

Newborn Falling Asleep 10

A Bright Spot 11

Time 13

Colic 14

Fused Acorns 15

This Time is Over 17

Pear 18

Raccoon 19

A Message 20

This is Different 21

Paracme 22

Another New Year 23

Greener Grass 24

Tall Grasses 25

In the Garden 26

Wheat Fields 27

Cicadas and Geraniums 28

If I Would Have Known 30

No Baby Books 31

Walking with my Husband 32

A Good Day 33

To Settle

in September in grass blades, a daffodil bulb,
a tapered hole, stringy roots dangling at my wrist.
Have I settled? I look into the hole,

I imagine a pig rooting for truffles,
his snout pushing up ridges of earth to expose
layers of clay and mud and silt and sand,

and not pretty cotton candy sand
that as a child I layered in a glass bottle,
more like dust that nestles in grooves between planks

of the knotted wood floor, or settling
into a chair, moss green mohair, chamomile tea
on the table, thick with honey. We are settling

into our house. A yellow light shines from the window
and there is a small barrel off the porch where I will
plant red geraniums and sweet potato vine.

Close

I wonder at times if I really know
you standing there grinding the coffee beans

while I stand here touching this window.
Then you bring me a sweet, or take

all the bundles from my arms. Your hand
is at my elbow even before my ankle twists

on the ice and I realize again that we are
the damp leaves cleaved together,

we are the imprint in new snow
as well as the body that just left it.

Rising

I have spent this trimester looking out
the skylight above the bed. The branches of a silver maple
fashion a lace against the sky, but today the window is covered
with a heavy quilt of snow.

So I bake all day. I cover the counter
with yeast and flour and I fold bread dough and stir batter,
I eat dough, my daughter eats dough, and my husband has a
  cookie
with his afternoon coffee.

In the evening I don't read. There is a nice weight
to the white coverlet over the mound of my belly that rises and
  falls
with each breath. On the dresser blue shadows grow deep
behind perfume bottles, like a jaunty party in tableau.

Nesting

The window shade is pulled in the nursery,
I go out to the stoop and brush my hair.

I watch the busy sparrow carrying
rootlets and grasses to the eave.

I go out and come back, shopping bags
dangle from my wrist, I go out and come back

with a trinket for the shelf.
I wear a path like a deer in the woods,

cupped depressions in the soft March mud.
Soon baby songbirds will stretch their white throats and bleat,

their feathers tucked inside a good nest
made from twigs and a few strands of blonde hair.

The Wrong Picture

A walk along the lake on wet grass after a deep rain
and I see a woman picnicking with her husband,
    their baby asleep
in the carriage, red gingham tablecloth, iced chardonnay,
yes, the whole thing.

He is animated standing telling a story, the water sparkles
    from behind,
she wears a wide brimmed hat, and her knees
are folded beneath her.

You never feel you are the pretty mother in a white nightgown
nursing the baby, with the sun filling
the fabric from behind.

No, I will not pick up that snapshot for the album,
with this baby I will sleep while I can,
crumbs on the counter,

and let myself cry into the baby's hair.

Birth

It all leads to this—
chalk arrows on the sidewalk
broken twigs on a forest path
bread crumbs in the bright snow

It is all I've thought of
fears stitched into apron hems
corked into perfume bottles
and whispered into bread dough

I clutch this starched sheet
a deep guttural bellow
like the lowest baritone
or the C string on the cello

Birth II

she is born
slick as wet pasta
barely drained
the clang
of the scissors
in the metal bowl

A Round

Dedicated to Bonnie Joyce Ruzicka
October 14, 1924- August 7, 2007

The baby is dressed in an ivory frock dotted with violets.

The old ladies pass her around, their skin tinged like spilled tea.

Freckled lilies encircle the coffin of satin.

And death looks like too much powder.

The baby extends one arm, one fist, and slowly uncurls each
    doughy finger,

a gesture wanting something from me, I think,

or perhaps it is the open

clean palm of an offer.

Sweet Milk Days

Inside the snow globe
I rock the baby
my feet on a braid of oval rug
and we are translucent
in lamplight that catches
the dust floating in the room
and around my hair.

Everything smells like milk
even the winter sky
is the color of milk.

Peering in, through soaped glass,
with a gold handbag
slung over lantern sleeves,
I once thought
how bland, and clicked away
through the cold light
of new snow.

Newborn Falling Asleep

Honey afternoon light hums
through the faded window shade.

Impossible for you to lie alone,
your bird body flutters next to mine.

On the sun filled porch is my book
and chamomile tea.

                              Please fall asleep.

Instead you wind like a mink around my neck
Gold curls cloak my chest,

and you try and return to the sound of my heart
as it hums through the fluids of my body.

A Bright Spot

Husband,

there is a speck of gold paint
on this old throw rug

from when we painted
that first living room,

that tiny apartment,
we drank beer,

listened to Patsy Cline, and you
reached all the high corners.

I am glad part
of that summer day

is here in this house,
the bright fleck

on the rug, while outside
it is white again,

so there is no horizon,
snow and sky blend.

We sit here eating
bowls of blueberries

and strawberries,
the bright juice stains

the yogurt, as we watch
out the window

more and more
snow fall.

Time

The dark space between the radiator ribs
has a blue tinge like the milk lolling
down the baby's cheek and time has this type of haziness too
like soaped glass.

The fan hums
a constant lullaby and the sun passes through the room
to play its shadow stretching game
upon the blue walls that fade to gray.

Colic

It is not quite the curdled milk on the wall,
or the screams that mute themselves so that my ears ring
like leaving a show, and walking out into the fall Chicago air.

It is the fear that it is not colic, that should leave her body,
like some sort of exorcism, head turned to the side, tongue slack
in the corner of her tiny baby mouth.

What if month four, month five, passes by
and she is still sour like pickles,
like kraut, like old limes.

Fused Acorns

I had hoped never to write about my children
especially this one I now call my eldest, especially

at this time when there is a pause before I even call her a child
especially about this, the blurred line where I end

and she begins. On walks when she was little
she collected fused acorns and she would clap her hands

at the egg cracked into the blue bowl, that released two yolks
from one shell. She loved duplexes, small loveseats,

and tandem bicycles. Once she found two trees wrapped
around one another, not competing for sunlight, but finding

a way to share it. I did nothing to discourage this. She was
my date to dinner parties drawing a smile from the host

with her linen napkin across her tiny lap. At the movies
we ate only the green M&M's by the light of the projector

and she always slept with her bare toes poking into my
    stomach.
How is it then that she has handled this cleave of a second child

with the grace of moonlight? While I stumble around feeling
like an amputee picking at the cracks in sidewalks

looking for fused acorns.

This Time is Over

The metal scoop in the flour, the open newspaper
by the bed, the pink rubber duck floats
in the morning bath.

We trace the shapes frost makes
on this side of the pane, the silver lines
crochet our images together.

The watch is still in the drawer.
Today the slanted sun could mean
midmorning or late afternoon.

But the red flag is up on the mailbox,
and even in the snow,
the bell on the door clangs.

Pear

The green pear on the wood shelf will be cut, later
I will rub the spots off the wine glass with linen

but now it is the quiet of glass and of mirrors that
show this haunted face that I once found interesting

and I grieve for what is lost. I fear the placidness
of this gray time, its lack of embroidery, and all

I can talk about now is the white landscape,
and the white sky, and if one is not careful,

how disorienting it is to look at everything
at once. I look to the pear, that I will later cut,

its brown freckles and crooked stem, this one pear,
it will soon be absorbed, and it will be gone.

Raccoon

Coming home, the screen door bangs
behind us. Ripped bags of groceries spill
lettuce and French dressing to the floor.

A handbag, sunglasses, a diaper bag
full of spit-upon clothes, a crying baby
I can do nothing but hand by the armpits

to her father and walk back out the door.
In the fresh air I release my hands from my hair,
walk in the middle of the street then down the tracks

tippy and tired, an S curve of a walk, taking
in the jagged breath of the weary. A raccoon
looks at me with the bandit mask of a costume ball,

the second one I have seen in broad daylight this week.
Possible distemper I am told, flooded from their homes.
Careful! They may feel brave and loopy,

they could be dangerous after trying to go home
and finding it so different from what it was.

A Message

Rain pours down in sheets.
The bird bath is flooded.
The streets are flooded.

When it stops it is quiet,
a yellow kind of quiet.

I fold a small paper boat,
with half of a poem
and a toothpick as the sail.

I place it afloat
outside my front door.

This is Different

This is different than a nervous breakdown,

yet still vulnerable like:
a photograph taken of someone sleeping,
or girlhood undergarments on the clothesline.

Who am I today:
wisps of air,
bottled sea foam,
jars of sunlight.

I try on *aimless* as a title:
a rabid animal,
a reaction to penicillin,
walking, the first day out to sea.

I focus on the water
draining clean down the stainless steel sink,
the vinaigrette separates after shaking,

and the canister of flour has already settled again.

Paracme

The point at which one is past one's prime.
-The Oxford English Dictionary

A just-soft pear,
so that one's hand
leaves a print

in the snow I found
Christmas tinsel
in the dark month of February

muddy boot-prints
crossed the bleached-
white kitchen tile

in the produce section
there was a couple fighting
I haven't seen since their wedding

day of peonies, their prime
spent last Tuesday,
so that now their heavy heads

bent forward to rest
against the ground.

Another New Year

We have always gone for a walk
on New Year's Day but this year we didn't.
I could scratch the frost on the inside
of the window. We move around each other

in the winter light but our eyes are on the floor.
You speak *who?* and I say *iron*
with the resolve of steel. Today it is snowing
side-ways again but we must go out. This time

you take my hand and tuck it
inside your elbow. You close the car door
careful that the hem of my skirt is on the inside.

Greener Grass

I spend a lot of time moving the glassware
around the top-rack trying to make it all fit.

Outside I notice the earth has thawed,
the garbage hidden under the snow is now exposed:

a beer can, a lost piece of mail, a Styrofoam package
from ground beef, and I see the fat robin,

and he of course has something dangling from his mouth.
I know it will be trash, something not natural caught in his beak,

something that will later seep into my dream,
the robin with the green plastic straw, or the Christmas tinsel.

But no, in fact, it is a worm
he has just plucked from the sidewalk

and I am somehow amazed that robins
still go about this business

of eating worms in the spring.

Tall Grasses

We are up too early and we leave the cats
still curled like little cushions on the porch chairs.

She is in the stroller and sees the woodpecker
before she hears it, and then there it is: knock, knock, knock.

She waves to the bird, hand open,
then closed, now just playing in a ray of light,

she kicks to relish the sun a little more. My coffee
is so full of flavor, this morning as bright as water,

with this child, my newest daughter, who helps me to
enjoy my life, who says *uaah,* almost under her breath

as she watches tall grasses and how they sway,
and I think no, it is not exactly the enjoyment

she helps me with,
it is the noticing.

In the Garden

It must have been June with the vase of magenta peonies
on the wood table. Tiny ants crawled furiously about
the unopened buds trying to quicken the flower's opening.

I love peonies, the earnest way they give it their all, a huge show,
and then they are spent. But yes, we were in the garden
and on the table was the vase of peonies.

You, my only daughter then, on the swing floating by us,
kicking up your legs, your hair a tail behind you,
puffs of laughter at what your step-father was saying.

Today we are in the garden again, but now the baby
is asleep upstairs, the monitor crackles with static
in the summer air. This time we are each in our own separate

place, the three of us together, you again on the swing, a year
older. From time to time you put your foot down in the dirt
and sway just slightly to the side. Our timelines have unrolled

like three satin ribbons, and we are each somewhere different
than we thought we would be, even though he is again roasting
the vegetables and you arranged the linens, bright upon the table.

I smell the lilacs still on the tree so it must be May
but a few of the antique plumes are brown and curling,
and in just days, perhaps, the peonies will bloom again.

Wheat Fields

In the story of *The Little Prince*, the wind blown wheat fields
   forever remind the fox
of his beloved prince, because of the sameness of the grain to
   the prince's golden hair.

I think of that story today, riding in the passenger seat,
watching the silent ticking of the rows of corn
   pass by my window.

But it is the open fields dotted with bales of hay where I smell
   my baby. The hay is sweet
and grassy, and somehow the same scent as the rub of
   applesauce, toast, sweat, and her neck

that now will always come to mind when we drive in the country
in early August and smell the fresh-mowed hay.

Cicadas and Geraniums

The cicadas are working up their loudest hum
fall is almost here, I know because the bite
in the air each morning makes me think of baking

bread or apple muffins but lately any change
brings a bit of sadness like the awareness that summer
will turn to fall even though the corn is at its full crunch

and the baby pulls up on the table leg, teeters there,
then sits back down, she is close to walking,
    and I am not yet ready
to plant bulbs, seeing how the flat of geraniums

has been sitting on the stoop since May,
    and I think I am here now
in this moment, but always realizing what was forgotten earlier
and chewing my nail about what is coming next

I know when I am like this I should take a moment
to sit in the garden, but when I am like this
I often don't want to be alone with my thoughts

but I also don't want to plant the geraniums
it just seems too pathetic that they would only
border the garden for a few weeks, so somehow

leaving the plants in their little plastic beds

to shrivel and wilt seems better than going out

where the cicadas' shrill reminds me that summer is ending.

If I Would Have Known

how this would all turn out

or is turning still,

spindle of an axis

unspooling all my thread,

I would not move the garden mulch

back to the mound,

each chunk of bark

and broken stick.

I would not unknead the bread,

the yeast would still fall

from the measuring spoon.

I would not glue the ends

of leaves back to the branch.

And on that October night,

I would not push up the rain,

flat against my palms,

I would still lean over you,

in our bed, my hair a curtain

around our faces.

No Baby Books

I can't paste little corners
to hold the photos
I'm sorry, I just can't.

What I will do instead,
for you my girls,
is to fold a fleet
of tiny paper ships
and set them out to sail,

and when you are grown,
and on the other side
of the pond, you may
unfold them one by one.

Please sit on the bench
close enough
to dip your toes
in the water
while you read
by then
this creased history.

Walking with my Husband

You push the stroller and I am saying
over-due thank you cards, the basil in the herb garden.

It is a moment not really raised on the relief map,
a necessary walk with a baby plucked from the floor.

I notice you watching the gardens. Purple cornflowers
and Queen Anne's Lace wave to our passing,

but it is the sunflowers to which you give your attention,
turning your head to follow each yellow face.

I am surprised it is these giants that you find beautiful,
not the black-eyed Susans in their party bunch,

or the butterfly milkweed that is at the level
of my hand to pet as we pass.

It is always new to me again that what we see
is not the same, that this moment, this walk

in this garden with the nodding sunflowers
may be a memory that you keep.

A Good Day

Please pick some mint for the melon salad, I say
and she goes out happy with the task to find a good sprig.

The baby is in the bath, her father will bring her,
wrapped in a white towel, to tell me how she laughed

at the duck floating in the water. This day is bright
as soda water, clean as vinegar, crisp as ginger root,

and we will end it by taking the baby's chair
out into the grass so we may eat together in the garden.

Apprentice House
Annual Chapbook Competition
Submission Guidelines

Apprentice House is the country's only campus-based, student-staffed book publisher. Directed by professors and industry professionals, it is a nonprofit activity of the Communication Department at Loyola College in Maryland. The Apprentice House model creates an unprecedented collaborative environment among faculty and students.

Apprentice House: the future of publishing...today!

The poetry chapbook contest is for poets previously unpublished in book form. Winner receives $250 prize and 20 copies. There is a $20 submission fee payable to Apprentice House. The annual deadline is April 1 postmark. Submit at least thirty pages of typed poetry manuscript. Mail to:

Chapbook Contest
Apprentice House
c/o Communication Department
Loyola University Maryland
4501 N. Charles St.
Baltimore, MD 21210.

Contact Apprentice House for complete guidelines at info@apprenticehouse.com or 410-617-5265.

The future of publishing...today!

Apprentice House is the country's only campus-based, student-staffed book publishing company. Directed by professors and industry professionals, it is a nonprofit activity of the Communication Department at Loyola College in Maryland.

Using state-of-the-art technology and an experiential learning model of education, Apprentice House publishes books in untraditional ways. This dual responsibility as publishers and educators creates an unprecedented collaborative environment among faculty and students, while teaching tomorrow's editors, designers, and marketers.

Outside of class, progress on book projects is carried forth by the AH Book Publishing Club, a co-curricular campus organization supported by Loyola College's Office of Student Activities.

Student Project Team for *Nesting*:
> Kaitlyn Lavelle, '10
> Kelsey Schaible, '11
> Amy M. Scioscia, '12

To learn more about Apprentice House books or to obtain submission guidelines, please visit www.ApprenticeHouse.com.

Apprentice House
Communication Department
Loyola University Maryland
4501 N. Charles Street
Baltimore, MD 21210
Ph: 410-617-5265 • Fax: 410-617-2198

www.ingramcontent.com/pod-product-compliance
Lightning Source LLC
Chambersburg PA
CBHW071438040426
42445CB00012BA/1388